Contents

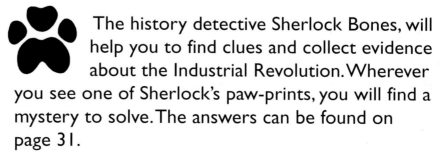

Words in **bold** can be found in the glossary on page 30

The history detective Sherlock Bones, will help you to find clues and collect evidence about the Industrial Revolution. Wherever you see one of Sherlock's paw-prints, you will find a mystery to solve. The answers can be found on page 31.

What was the Industrial Revolution?

The word revolution means 'upheaval' or 'great change'. The revolution that happened during the eighteenth and nineteenth centuries was so amazing that it didn't just change Britain, it changed the whole world.

Until about 1780 Britain was an overwhelmingly rural country. This meant that the vast majority of people lived in the countryside. They lived off the land by growing crops and rearing animals.

Britain has been described as being local or regional at this time. This meant that most people had little knowledge or experience of other places outside their region. This was because it was difficult to travel around. Roads were bad and travel expensive, uncomfortable and slow. Each region of Britain had its own city, market town and a port where goods were traded.

In the 1750s, the population of Britain was very small – about 6 million – and only one-fifth of people lived in towns. By 1851, the population had tripled to nearly 20 million and more than half of

This picture shows the powerful iron furnaces at Coalbrookdale, Shropshire glowing in the night.

THE HISTORY DETECTIVE INVESTIGATES

The Industrial Revolution

Peter Hicks

WAYLAND

The History Detective series:
The Celts
Anglo-Saxons
Tudor Exploration
Tudor Home
Tudor Medicine
Tudor Theatre
Tudor War
The Civil Wars
Victorian Crime
Victorian Factory
Victorian School
Victorian Transport
Local History
The Industrial Revolution
Post-War Britain

First published in 2008 by Wayland

This paperback edition published in 2010 by Wayland

Wayland
338 Euston Road
London NW1 3BH

Wayland Australia
Level 17/207 Kent Street
Sydney, NSW 2000

Editor: Camilla Lloyd
Designer: Simon Borrough
Picture researcher: Shelley Noronha
Cartoon artwork: Richard Hook

Picture Acknowledgments: The author and publisher would like to thank the following for their pictures to be reproduced in this publication: Cover photographs: Main: The Art Archive/Science Museum London/Eileen Tweedy, right: Wayland Picture Library; AKG: Sotheby's/akg-images: 7; Art Archive: Science Museum London/Eileen Tweedy, Culver Pictures: 18, Science Museum London/Eileen Tweedy: 19 (b), Institution of Civil Engineers/Eileen Tweedy: 22 (t), Eileen Tweedy: 23, John Meek: 25; Peter Hicks: 1, 5 (t), 9 (t), 10, 13, 15 (both), 16, 20 (b), 27, 28 (both), 29; Topfoto: World History Archive: 4, World History Archive: 5 (b), World History Archive: 6 (t), World History Archive: 11 (b),

HIP/Oxford Science Archive: 12 (t), World History Archive: 12 (b), Fotomas: 20 (t), World History Archive: 21, Topfoto: 24 (t), Fotomas: 24 (b), Topfoto: 26, Whitehorne/Topfoto: 27; Wayland Picture Library: 6 (b), 8, 9 (b), 17 (both), 19 (t), 22 (background).

British Library Cataloguing in Publication Data:
Hicks, Peter, 1952-
    The Industrial Revolution. - (The history detective investigates)
    1. Industrial revolution - History - Juvenile literature
    I. Title
    909.8'1

ISBN: 978 0 7502 6350 4

Printed in China

Wayland is a division of Hachette Children's Books, an Hachette UK company
www.hachette.co.uk

Britain did make things before the revolution. For centuries, industry had existed but it was on a small scale. Until the 1780s, Britain's industry was mainly focused on making woollen cloth. This work took place in homes and sometimes involved whole families and was called the **domestic system**. Merchants delivered raw wool and took away the woven cloth. A completely different system took over after 1780, which involved people going to work in the factories outside the home. This was called the **factory system**.

What brought about these changes? Britain had become an industrial country. It stopped relying on farming and agriculture for its wealth and began to make or manufacture things in factories. The things that were made in Britain were sold at home and abroad. In this book, we will investigate how and why this revolution happened.

Before the Industrial Revolution, Britain had an iron industry but it was small scale.

Looking at the furnaces and the mine, how was industry changing the landscape?

With the increased demand for coal during the Industrial Revolution, mines became a common sight.

Why did the Industrial Revolution happen in Britain?

The causes of Britain's industrialization were all in place by the late eighteenth century. For example, important changes to land and agriculture had taken place. Land was bought up by individual farmers and enclosed into bigger parcels of land called farms. This allowed the richer farmers to experiment and try out new crops and animal breeds.

Reaping machines helped harvests to be collected much more quickly.

Jethro Tull's seed drill (left) helped to increase the size of the harvests.

Improved farming methods meant a better and more plentiful diet. This helped the population to increase as people lived longer. More people meant a bigger workforce who needed to buy things, so demand for products like food, clothes and shoes rose dramatically.

Britain was becoming much richer financially. This wealth came from a number of sources. Britain had an empire and countries such as India, within this empire, were very valuable because they provided **raw materials**, overseas markets and industries and products of their own. The slave trade took off in the eighteenth century and slaves were bought with British exports. The slave trade made vast profits for merchants who dealt in ships, tobacco, cotton and sugar from countries within the empire.

🐾 Bristol's quays on the River Avon are crowded. What do you think had to be built to cope with the large number of ships?

Developments in transport also helped trade and industry to grow. For example, better roads were being built which allowed people to travel around and goods to be transported to other places. Improvements in transport also allowed communication to develop and ideas to spread. A network of canals meant that **bulky** goods, particularly coal, could be carried long distances cheaply.

Religion also helped Britain industrialize. Although, Britain was a Christian country in the eighteenth century, only members of the Christian **Church of England** were allowed to enter the universities. **Dissenting** Christian groups that were separate from the Church of England, such as Quakers, Unitarians and Presbyterians often entered trade, industry or science instead of going to university. Scientific inventions and successful traders and businessmen helped British industry progress.

DETECTIVE WORK

Look on the back of the new £20 note. Who can you see? Find out why this man's ideas helped Britain's Industrial Revolution. Why is he so interested in pin making?

Bristol was a wealthy port because of its trade with America and its share in the slave trade.

Why was power so important in the revolution?

Before the industrial revolution, wind, water and horses provided energy power. The trouble was that these sources were often unreliable. The wind didn't always blow, rivers often dried up in the summer and not everyone could afford a horse.

Inventors tried to develop a source of power that was cheap, plentiful and not dependant on the weather. In 1698, Thomas Savery invented a steam engine that was improved ten years later by Thomas Newcomen. Newcomen's machine – known as a 'fire engine' – wasn't perfect as it used a lot of coal. However, it was useful for pumping out flood water from mines. Another problem with the fire engine was that its action – a beam moving up and down – limited what the engine could be used for.

In 1769, the inventor, James Watt, developed a 'steam condenser', which allowed the engine to use much less fuel and that made it cheaper to run. Then, in 1781, Watt found that if he attached a rod to the cross-beam and placed a small cog rotating around a bigger one ('sun and planet' gears) it could drive wheels. This was a

DETECTIVE WORK

Find out how a steam engine works. What are its principles? See if there are any models of steam engines in a local museum. Watch out for summer steam fairs. See a working steam engine at www.hooknorton brewey. co.uk

This picture shows the famous rotary engine developed by James Watt (1736-1819).

This painting shows a powerful steam hammer shaping a bar of red-hot iron.

What dangers do you think might have faced the men working in a foundry like the one on the left?

This plan shows James Watt's 'Sun and Planet' engine.

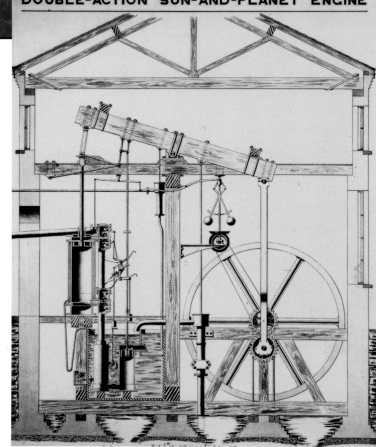

JAMES WATT 1788
DOUBLE-ACTION SUN-AND-PLANET ENGINE

crucial discovery because now steam engines could power the new spinning machines in the big cotton mills that were previously water-powered. These 'rotary' engines were used in iron works, coal and copper mines (to winch or lift miners up the shafts), on canals for raising barges and pumping water, breweries, brick works and china factories.

With the popularity of the steam engines came a huge demand for the coal that was used as fuel. As a result, industries sprung up on the coal fields of the Midlands, the North of England, Scotland and South Wales so they could be near the source of their power. The coal industry was transformed because steam needed a constant supply of coal. More and more mines were dug to meet the massive demand for coal.

What was it like in a factory?

A spinning mill in operation. Can you see the small girl cleaning the machinery?

The factory system that came about during the Industrial Revolution was much more efficient than the domestic system. The machines and workforce were all in one place and everybody inside the factory had their own particular job to do. The textile industry was the first to take advantage of steam-driven machines. They used steam to manufacture cotton cloth with machines for combing, spinning and later with the power looms for weaving cloth.

Factory fines

'Any spinner found with his window open — 1s (5p)
Any spinner found washing himself — 1s (5p)
Any spinner leaving his oil can out of its place — 6d (2½p)
Any spinner putting his gas out too soon — 1s (5p)
Any spinner spinning with his gas light too long in the morning — 2s (10p)
Any spinner heard whistling — 1s (5p)
Any spinner being five minutes late after the last bell rings — 2s (10p)
Any spinner being sick and cannot find another Spinner to give satisfaction, to pay for steam, per day — 6d (2½p)'

William Cobbett's Political Register, Volume II, on 20th November 1824, listed the fines that were used to punish factory workers in the nineteenth century.

What were conditions like in these factories? Powered by steam and lit by gas light, they were noisy, dusty and unbearably hot in the summer. The **shifts** were long, often 15 to 16 hours a day. This wasn't unusual for people worked long hours in the domestic system too, but the discipline inside the factory was tough, sometimes harsh. Once the men, women and children started work, usually at 5 or 6 o'clock in the morning, the pace and pressure of the work and the dangerous machinery made for an exhausting and unsafe workplace. The men in charge, called 'overseers', were very strict and workers could be fined for breaking the rules. A spinner whistling or leaving his window open to get some air resulted in a 5p fine. That was a big chunk out of a weekly wage of between 50p and £1.

Some children were sent to work by parents needing to increase the family income. For young children the factories must have been frightening places. Orphans were also sent as **apprentices** from the **workhouses**. Small children were popular with factory owners because they were paid lower wages than adults and because they were so small they could clean machines while they were still running, and this saved the factory owner money.

DETECTIVE WORK

Cotton replaced wool as the most popular cloth in Britain. Where did Britain import cotton from? Why was it so popular?
Find out why Lancashire was the home of cotton production throughout the Industrial Revolution.

The noise created inside the textile mills was deafening.

Other workplaces were also dangerous and tough. Victorian workshops, forges and **sweatshops** of all sizes were often overcrowded and poorly **ventilated**. In these conditions, the goods of the Industrial Revolution: bricks, iron, ropes, chains, glass, china and cloth, were churned out.

Children carried lumps of clay in the brickyard. The dust was very dangerous to their young lungs.

What was it like in a coal mine?

An older girl pulls a heavy coal truck helped by two younger children in a Scottish coal mine, 1848.

In the early 1700s, the coal industry was of little importance to Britain. It produced only 2 million tonnes a year. Most of this was used in people's homes for heating although some was exported.

Coal later became the main fuel that allowed the Industrial Revolution to take off. Demand increased dramatically because of steam power and also because of Abraham Darby's discovery that iron could be **smelted** using coke, which comes from coal. Deeper and more dangerous mines were dug and by 1825, Britain was mining 50 million tonnes a year.

With so many mines opening there was a shortage of labour so women and children as well as men were encouraged to 'work down the pit'. These places were incredibly dangerous. The men, women and children working underground faced explosions, flooding, cave-ins and pit falls, as well as many medical conditions, such as lung diseases.

This painting shows an anxious woman waiting to see if her husband, a victim of a mine explosion, is alive or dead.

DETECTIVE WORK

The Davy Lamp is sometimes called the 'safety lamp'. Find out the scientific principle that makes it work. What other methods did miners use to detect dangerous gases? See if you can find some miners lamps in junk or antique shops or local museums.

🐾 **Why do you think the picture of the Scottish coal mine (page 12, top) shocked Victorian Britain?**

The biggest threat when working in a coal mine came from explosions caused by the use of fire in the pits. The dreaded 'fire-damp' or methane gas was often ignited by the candles and steel spark mills that were used for lighting. When Humphrey Davy's safety lamp was introduced in 1816, it encouraged pit owners to send miners into even deeper and more dangerous parts of the mine.

Women carried coal baskets up many flights of ladders or dragged full tubs of coal. Children, sometimes as young as 4 or 5 years old, were used as 'trappers', meaning that they had to open and close trap doors to control the air supply or ventilation in the mine. In 1841, William Wardle called mining 'the hardest work under heaven'.

This is a miner's safety lamp. At first miners did not like them because the light was poor and they still used dangerous candles.

How did transport improve?

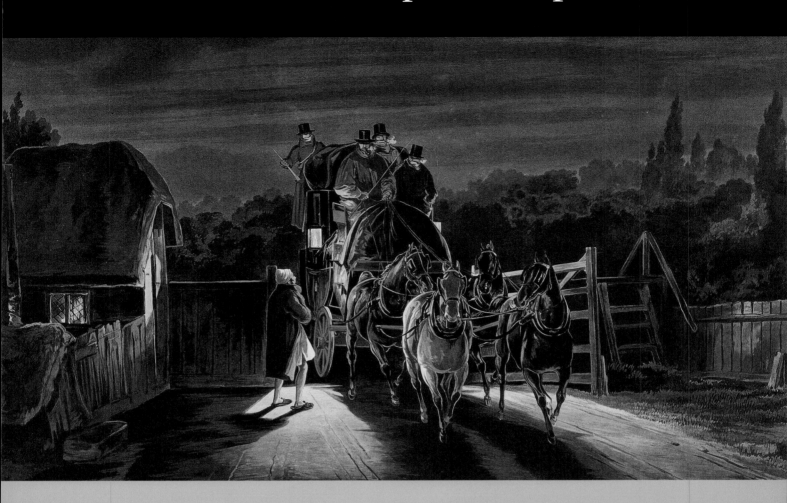

Eighteenth century roads were very poor and hardly used. Local areas had to look after their stretches of road but rarely did. In the winter rain they became seas of mud. River transport was often disrupted in the summer because rivers were so shallow that barges and boats couldn't use them.

Roads slowly improved, mainly because of 'Turnpike Trusts'. Groups of local businessmen would raise funds, gain permission from an Act of Parliament, then adopt and improve a stretch of road and charge people who travelled along it. The Trust built toll houses with gates at each end where the travellers had to pay to use the roads and this money could be put towards more road improvements. Although the turnpike network did improve journey times and mail and news travelled faster, the conditions of the roads varied and sending bulky goods by wagon or packhorse was still costly.

This painting shows a coach passing through the turnpike gate having paid the toll.

The Duke of Bridgewater was a coal owner in Worsley. The market for this coal was in Manchester which was eight miles from Worsley. Road transport had proved too expensive so the Duke decided to build a canal. By 1760, Parliament gave permission to begin construction. His canal designed by James Brindley crossed the River Irwell by an impressive **aqueduct** and tunnelled through two hills. It was such a success that it inspired a huge network of canals to be built over the next 70 years.

TABLE of TOLLS.

For every time they pass over this BRIDGE.

	s	d
For every Coach, Landau, Hearse, Chaise, Chair, or such like Carriages drawn by Six Horses, Mares, Geldings, or Mules.	2	0
Ditto ———— By Four Ditto ————	1	6
Ditto ———— by Two Ditto ————	1	0
Ditto ———— by One Ditto ————	0	6
For every Horse, Mule, Ass, pair of Oxen, Drawing or Harness'd to draw any Waggon, Cart, or such like carriage, for each Horse &c	0	3
For a Horse, Mule, or Ass, laden or unladen and not drawing	0	1½
For a Horse, Mule, or Ass carrying double	0	2
For an Ox, Cow, or neat cattle	0	1
For a Calf, Pig, Sheep, or lamb	0	0½
For every Horse, Mule, Ass, or carriage going on the roads and not over the Bridge, half the said tolls.		
For every Foot passenger, going over the Bridge	0	0½

N.B. This Bridge being private property, every Officer or Soldier, whether on duty or not, is liable to pay toll for passing over, as well as any baggage waggon, Mail-coach or the Royal Family.

The table of tolls required to cross the Ironbridge in Shropshire (see page 28).

The first canals followed the shape of the land and avoided hills, but later engineers like Thomas Telford constructed **locks** that allowed canals to climb the hills. Barges, pulled by horses could reach all the main industrial cities of Britain and link up the important rivers.

This transport 'revolution' cut the cost of transporting raw materials and goods and opened up new markets for farmers, traders and merchants. It helped industry because it didn't matter if factories were a long way from the customer. The canals could take goods to towns and cities all over Britain.

DETECTIVE WORK
Locks allowed barges to ascend and descend hills. Find out how a lock works. What did the boatman have to do to get his barge into the lock?

The impressive flight of locks at Caen Hill, Devizes, Wiltshire.

🐾 **What problems might lots of locks have caused for the boatmen?**

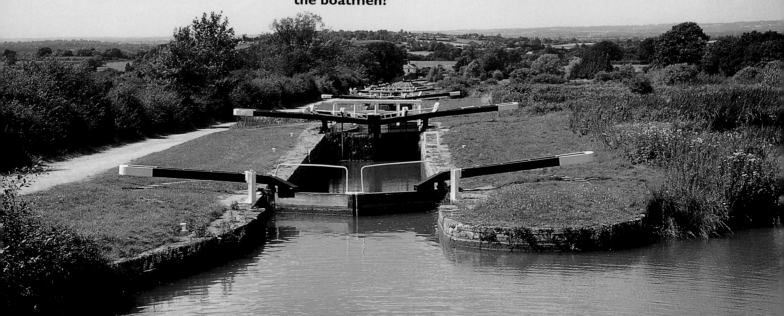

How did the railways change Britain?

Canals helped to improve British industry but there were drawbacks to the canal system. They were slow because of the many locks and goods often waited for weeks in crowded docks. With the canal owners charging high prices, people looked for an alternative. The alternative was the railway.

Railways and tramways were first used in mines and quarries where horses and humans pulled the wagons. Once steam power was applied industrialists saw the advantages of railways for both goods and passengers. With the opening of the first railways from Stockton to Darlington in 1825 and Liverpool to Manchester in 1830, they became an immediate success. Manchester businessmen managed to save £20,000 in transport costs in 6 months! By 1851, 10,780 km (6,700 miles) of track had been laid by a team of navigators ('navvies'). They built the cuttings, embankments, bridges, tunnels and viaducts from earth and bricks that transformed the landscape.

DETECTIVE WORK

Although in time the railways were accepted, many people objected to the construction. Find out some of the arguments against the railways and why the opposition often came from the coach or canal companies. When a huge city station was built why did working people suffer?

The amazing Ouse Valley viaduct on the London to Brighton railway line. Built in 1841, its 37 arches contain 11 million bricks.

The railway network had enormous effects on the Industrial Revolution and on Britain. The boost to industry with the demand for iron, coal, bricks, timber, gravel and steam engines was huge and many factory owners made vast fortunes. People had to be employed to build and work on the railways. The speedy transport of raw materials and goods brought costs down and new markets were created. Farmers, for example, could send their produce to new markets in the cities by train.

Excited spectators cheer the opening of the Stockton to Darlington Railway, 1825.

Improvements in travel also changed the way people lived. Crowded cities grew larger because stations served the new areas that were springing up as the towns grew. Seaside towns became popular, either with working people's day trips on Sundays or with the wealthy who could stay for a fortnight in the summer. Above all, the population became more mobile. In 1851, more than 6 million people travelled from all over Britain to see the Great Exhibition in London's Hyde Park (right). A new travel agent called Thomas Cook organized special return trains to London and the idea of tourism started to develop.

Queen Victoria opened the Great Exhibition in May, 1851.

Why were engineers so important to the revolution?

Inventors in this period, played an important role in the development of industry. The ideas and inventions of talented and creative engineers allowed technology to improve and British industry to grow and become more efficient.

The great George Stephenson gives orders to one of the train drivers.

James Watt is known as 'The Father of the Industrial Revolution'. He was not only a great inventor but also by teaming up with the industrialist Matthew Boulton, he became a successful supplier of steam engines to industries. By 1800, Boulton, who said: 'I sell, sir, what all the world desires – power', had sold over 200 Boulton and Watt steam engines across Britain.

Builders of huge projects, known as **civil engineers**, made a great contribution to Britain's new infrastructure. Thomas Telford, a talented road builder constructed the London to Holyhead road (the A5) with his magnificent **suspension bridge** over the Menai Straits that opened in 1825. Telford also built canals and his Pont Cysyllte aqueduct over the River Dee is a masterpiece of engineering. The aqueduct has nineteen arches that carry an iron channel for barges 35 metres (116 feet) above the valley.

DETECTIVE WORK

In your school or local library, find out about the wars that Britain fought between 1770 and 1815. How did war affect Britain's economy and the iron industry especially? Why did war increase the demand for iron?

The Britannia Railway Bridge crossing the Menai Straits, Wales. It was designed by George's son, Robert.

There were engineering heroes in the building of the railways. George Stephenson, 'The Father of the Railway,' was responsible for the Stockton to Darlington railway. George was helped by his son, Robert and won the Rainhill Trials of 1829 with the 'Rocket', which opened the Liverpool to Manchester Railway in 1830.

Probably the most successful of all the engineers was Isambard Kingdom Brunel. He built tunnels, bridges and steamships like the 'Great Britain' steamship, now restored in its home port of Bristol. Brunel is probably best remembered for building the Great Western Railway that linked London's Paddington Station with Bristol and the West Country.

🐾 Why do you think so many sightseers turned up to see the Britannia Bridge being built?

George Stephenson's 'Rocket', in the Science Museum, London.

What was life like in the cities?

One of the biggest problems caused by the Industrial Revolution was the severe overcrowding in towns and cities. The number of people living in towns and cities as opposed to the rural areas increased greatly. This process in known as urbanization. Industrial centres grew by three or four times. Many people moved to towns and cities because they offered jobs, higher wages, shops, markets and leisure interests for the workers. This rise in population put great pressure on housing. People were often crammed in poorly-built, damp, unhygienic houses in the cheapest, dirtiest and smelliest parts of town. These areas were called slums.

Deepening the sewer below Fleet Street, London, 1845.

DETECTIVE WORK

The man who pioneered the clean up of nineteenth century towns and cities was the civil engineer, Joseph Bazalgette. Find out what he did in London in the 1860s and why his work is never seen.

This is an example of the poor housing in British cities during the nineteenth century.

The cartoonist, George Cruikshank, shows how London was spreading outwards in 'London going out of town,' 1829.

In the cartoon, what things are running away from the builders or being destroyed?

Working class slums were unpleasant because the working classes were only able to pay very little **rent** as their wages from the factories were so low. They were also often **unemployed** and could fall behind with the rent. Some ran away without paying the rent at all. The profits from this type of housing were low so the builders made the housing very basic with cheap materials and without proper ventilation. Unsurprisingly, these conditions led to disease. In 1837, 59,000 people died of tuberculosis – an infectious lung disease made worse by cold, damp and dirty air.

Another health risk came from **slaughterhouses** that were usually built in heavily populated areas. The animals that went into these houses were quickly slaughtered. After butchering, the waste, intestines or **offal**, was thrown onto **dunghills** or into drains to rot. In the summer, the disgusting waste attracted plagues of flies.

The most serious problem with the overcrowding was poor **sanitation**. The lack of proper drains and sewers caused massive hygiene problems. Human sewage was dropped into cess-pits (which often overflowed when it rained), drains, dumps, streams and rivers, so clean drinking water was hard to find. If people drank water contaminated by raw sewage they risked disease, such as **cholera**, which was particularly deadly. There were cholera outbreaks in towns and cities throughout the nineteenth century. There were two serious **epidemics** in 1831-32 and 1848-49 that killed more than 76,000 people. Cities were not just dirty – they could kill you!

'One day I walked with one of these middle class gentlemen into Manchester. I spoke to him about the disgraceful unhealthy slums…the factory workers lived in. I declared I had never seen so badly built a town in my life. He listened patiently…and… remarked: "And yet there is a great deal of money made here. Good morning, Sir!"'

F.Engels wrote about the state of the working class slums in *The Condition of the Working Class in England*, in 1844.

Who benefited from the Industrial Revolution?

Historians often argue about whether the Industrial Revolution made things better or worse for the people in Britain. The changes that the revolution brought with it benefited some and cost others, for example the poorly paid workers in the factories suffered under poor working and living conditions.

Engineers like Robert Stephenson, (seated, centre) were the celebrities of the day because of their daring engineering. The Crystal Palace below was designed by Joseph Paxman and was the world's first iron and glass building.

The landowners benefited from Industrialization. If you owned good farmland and you modernized, great profits could be made from the growing markets in the cities. Some estates were so big that the landowner rented out land to tenant farmers and made a huge income from the rent. A landowner might even be lucky enough to discover coal under his land and his fortune was assured. If a canal or railway company wanted to build across his land he could get a lot of money for selling it.

Factory owners and industrialists making goods or providing services that people wanted often made money. A good example of this was Josiah Wedgwood. Born into a family of potters he saved enough money to open his own factory. Using the new technologies available he produced fine china for people who could afford it. His 'Queen's Ware' (as used by Royalty) was a great hit with the public.

Some skilled workers did well in the years of the Industrial Revolution. For engineers, who made, maintained and repaired the thousands of new steam engines, wages were high. They formed **trade unions** to protect their conditions at work and their wages. Workers like these were better off than the unskilled and poor labourers or workers. The better off workers could pay into 'friendly societies' and could save for their families. These organizations, for a few pennies a week, would help the worker and his family if he was sick or injured. There were no such things as social security or benefits at this time so people were very vulnerable and the unions could give them some protection and peace of mind.

This is a certificate of Trade Union Membership (1890). If a worker was a member of a skilled trained union he was doing well for himself.

> ### DETECTIVE WORK
> Coalbrookdale in Shropshire is often called 'the cradle of the Industrial Revolution'. What does this mean? Find out what Coalbrookdale made and the importance of the Darby family.

AMALGAMATED SOCIETY OF ENGINEERS, MACHINISTS, MILLWRIGHTS, SMITHS, AND PATTERN MAKERS.

BE UNITED AND INDUSTRIOUS

Who suffered in the years of the Industrial Revolution?

The small farmers were the first group to lose out in the eighteenth century with the onset of industrialization. They owned strips of land and grew different crops on them. Once the enclosure movement began, the richer farmers bought up these strips. Traditionally, the common or public land was left for the poor people to graze their cattle but some of this land was enclosed, too, as farming became mechanized. A new type of worker was created, the 'landless labourer'. Once he had sold his strips and spent the money that he had been paid, he had to try to seek work on the big farms.

This painting is called 'The Rick-Burner's cottage.' Poverty could drive people to desperate things.

The homeless and very poor often had to stay in asylums or night shelters like this one in Cripplegate, London (right).

Caption: At Playhouse Yard in Cripplegate, the Asylum for The Houseless Poor served those who could not even afford the 2-6 pence rate for a night in a lodging house. The applicants would gather in the yard outside the house where they were made to wait until 5.00 p.m., jockeying for a position at the front of the crowd. Credit: ©2005 Credit TopFoto / Fotomas

🐾 In the picture above, who is tempting the man in the cottage to burn down the farmer's hay stacks?

Technology was very important to the Industrial Revolution and it created lots of new jobs. However, it also put many people out of work too. The machines invented during the revolution replaced many labourers so less people were needed to work on the land and in the mills. Farm labourers lost their jobs to mechanical reapers and **threshing** machines. And many people found themselves without a job or an income. The handloom weavers also lost their jobs to machines. **Carding** and spinning were mechanized and power looms came in the 1830s and 1840s. Before then, textiles were woven by around 240,000 handloom weavers in cottages. Once mills adopted the power looms these weavers lost their jobs and experienced terrible hardship.

DETECTIVE WORK

Workhouse orphans who were apprenticed to factories and workshops often led a miserable life. Find out why Oliver Twist did not want to be apprenticed to Mr. Gamfield. Look up, in your school library *'Oliver Twist'* by Charles Dickens, Millennium Library edition, pages 16-21.

The poorest paid workers were the agricultural labourers in the countryside. Farmers close to industrial centres had to pay higher wages to keep their workers from going to the cities. Labourers in counties away from the cities received very low wages and suffered great poverty. Between 1833 and 1845, Dorset labourers were paid 38p a week compared to labourers in Northumberland (near Newcastle) who were paid 58p.

When times were really hard, people could apply for charity and many received soup, bread and blankets when unemployed during the long winters. For the old, physically and mentally ill and the orphans there were workhouses. After 1834, the government deliberately made conditions unpleasant so people wouldn't even enter them! For many, they were regarded as prisons and to be avoided at all costs. Life for the unskilled was a struggle.

'Go down into the villages...and then look at the miserable sheds in which the labourers reside [live]! Look at these hovels, made of mud and straw, bits of glass, or old, cast-off windows...merely stuck in the mud-wall. Enter them and look at...the rags on the backs of the wretched inhabitants.'

William Cobbett in *'Rural Rides'*, 1830, described the plight of the landless labourer.

A woman comforts her child at the St. Giles workhouse in London, 1877 or 1878.

Did anybody try to improve things?

Although Britain's transformation from a rural to a manufacturing economy made her the 'workshop of the world', many people were worried about the social costs. The harshness of work in factories and mines was ruining many people's lives, especially young children.

Some employers were advanced in their thinking and treated their workers well. Robert Owen's model mills near Glasgow (see page 27) had good working conditions, housing and education for the workforce. Many campaigners tried to improve factory conditions but met stiff resistance from the owners who were mostly interested in profit. They wanted to be left alone from government interference, this was called a **laissez-faire** approach, and did not want to be told how long their employees could work and what they had to be paid.

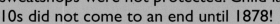

Lord Ashley (also called Lord Shaftesbury) campaigned tirelessly to improve conditions in mines and factories but it was a long struggle. In 1842, he helped to get the Mines Act passed in Parliament, which forbade women and children under the age of 10 from working underground. The House of Lords reduced it from 13 years old to 10 years old. Five years later, the campaign to cut working hours was successful. Ashley and the Ten Hours Movement campaigners pushed through Parliament the Ten Hours Bill and this limited women and children under 18 years old to 58 hours of work a week. It had taken 16 years to get that far. The law was tightened up to stop shifts going over 10 hours in 1850 and 1853. Of course, these laws only protected factory workers – many children who worked in workshops and sweatshops were not protected. Child labour for under 10s did not come to an end until 1878!

Lord Shaftesbury (1801-1885) was one of the many campaigners for better mine and factory conditions.

DETECTIVE WORK

When times were hard in the 1830s and 1840s a large group of people calling themselves the '**Chartists**' was formed. What were their aims and how did they try to persuade the government to improve things? Why do you think they failed?

Another reformer called Edwin Chadwick was horrified at the filthy conditions of the cities. He wrote a damning report in 1842 and a Public Health Act was passed in 1848. There was still a lot of resistance to cleaning up the cities and many landlords complained about the cost of improving conditions. It was to be another 25 years (and more deadly cholera epidemics) before the cities were cleaned up and proper underground sewers were put in.

Robert Owen's model village and mills, New Lanark, Scotland.

🐾 How do you think Oastler is trying to get a reaction out of his readers in his letter (right)?

SLAVERY IN YORKSHIRE

'*Thousands of little children, both male and female, but principally female, from SEVEN to fourteen years, are daily compelled to labour from six o'clock in the morning to seven in the evening with only – Britons, blush whilst you read it! – with only thirty minutes allowed for eating and recreation.*'

Richard Oastler complained about the conditions of the Yorkshire mills in a letter to the Leeds Mercury newspaper on 16 October, 1830.

Your project

Let's do some local detective work on the Industrial Revolution. There are lots of sites and artefacts to see, especially ones to do with the 'transport revolution'. People who locate and research these Industrial Revolution sites are called 'industrial archaeologists'. You, too, can look around at sites and show what you find in a presentation.

Topic Questions

- Find out how transport developed in your area and how it might have changed where you live. How did it affect local agriculture and industry?
- Visit your local library or second-hand book shop and look for old maps of your area. Can you see what changes have happened through time?
- Is there evidence of a turnpike road? Look for toll houses or gates, changes in the direction of roads, toll bridges, old country inns for evidence of where they might have been.
- Look for bridges that were built in the Industrial Revolution.
- Is there a canal near you? (either disused or working). Look for wharfs, locks, factories, changes to the nearby river, street patterns, public houses with relevant names e.g. The Barge Inn or Jolly Boatman.
- If you live near a port, visit the docks and see if you can find out when, why and how they were built. Was your port famous for a particular **cargo**?

The world's first iron bridge over the River Severn at Coalbrookdale, Shropshire.

This simple cottage is in fact an old toll house.

Project Ideas

- Find out when the railway came to your area. Think about why the builders chose the routes they did. Are the routes between main towns and cities? Are there cuttings, embankments, bridges or viaducts?
- Look at the stations in your area. Are there any original station buildings? Are there remains of branch lines to factories, mines or brickyards?
- You can use local directories to find out what trades and businesses grew up near the railway stations.
- Are there any houses that date from the time of the railway? For example, houses that may have been for the railway workers.

Project presentation

- Choose something about the Industrial Revolution that you find the most interesting. For example, you could look into the history of a famous inventor and could write a biography about him.
- Another fascinating area you could look into surrounds the men who built the railways. These men were called 'navvies', which was short for navigators. You can see how much of what they built is still here.
- When you go out to look for signs of industrialization: canals, railways and roads take a camera if you have one, a sketchpad and a pencil. You can take pictures and keep a record of how the Industrial Revolution changed the place where you live.

Glossary

apprentices Young people sent to employers to learn a trade.

aqueduct A man-made channel carrying water over a river valley.

bulky Something that takes up a lot of space and is usually heavy.

carding The combing of raw textiles like cotton or wool to make ready for spinning.

cargo Goods or products that are transported for trade or business.

Chartists People who campaigned for political and social change during the mid-nineteenth century.

cholera Highly infectious disease that can cause death.

Church of England The established or official Christian church of England.

civil engineer During the Industrial Revolution these engineers worked on public works projects.

dissenting Disagreeing with the official religion of the country.

domestic system An industry which includes people working from their homes, often part-time.

dunghills Heaps of animal waste.

enclosure movement Movement where land that had been common or shared was fenced off and bought by a single owner.

epidemic A serious outbreak of a disease that spreads quickly.

factory system An efficient system of making things that came into being in the Industrial Revolution. People worked in factories doing a particular job for a wage.

laissez-faire From the french 'leave be or leave alone', the view that governments should not interfere with businesses.

locks Short sections of a canal with gates at each end letting water in and out. Locks allow barges to go up and down hills.

loom A frame for weaving cloth.

offal The internal parts of a dead animal.

raw materials Any material from which something is made, for example, timber.

rent Regular payment for the use of land or buildings.

sanitation Keeping buildings and the water supply clean so that they do not spread disease.

shift A set period of time for work.

slaughterhouse The place where animals are killed and made into meat products.

social costs The price or suffering caused to people and society.

suspension bridge A bridge that hangs or suspends from cables or chains that hang between towers and are fixed at both ends.

smelted When rock is heated and melted to remove the metal from it.

sweatshop A place of work with poor conditions, for example, long hours and low pay.

trade unions An organization of workers. Through its leaders the union can talk to the employer on behalf of the workers.

threshing Hitting the ears of wheat to separate out the grain.

unemployed To be without a job and not earning money.

ventilated A building or room that has fresh air brought into it.

workhouse A place where people who could not support themselves could go to live and work. They were often strict and unpleasant.

Answers

Page 5:   Industry was polluting the air, causing damage to the land and creating industrial waste.

Page 6:   Docks had to be built to cope with the queues of ships entering Bristol.

Page 9:   The workers faced de-hydration, they inhaled smoke and could suffer with the heat or burn themselves.

Page 13:   Because children and young girls were working in such dangerous places and could get hurt.

Page 15:   The problem was that it took such a long time to pass through so many locks. This flight takes nearly two hours to climb!

Page 19:   Engineering works like this amazing bridge were considered to be wonders at this time.

Page 21:   Animals and haystacks are running away. Trees and fences are being destroyed.

Page 24:   The man is so poor that the devil is tempting him to take his misery out on the richer farmer by setting light to his harvest.

Page 27:   He is trying to make them feel ashamed and concerned. He writes that people should 'blush' hearing of the dreadful conditions.

Further Information

Books to read

Empire and Industry 1700-1900 by Ian Dawson (Oxford University Press, 2001)

Britain 1750-1900 by Nigel Kelly, Rosemary Rees and Jane Shuter (Heinemann, 1998)

All About the Industrial Revolution by Peter Hepplewhite and Mairi Campbell (Wayland, 2002)

The Industrial Revolution, Events and Outcomes by Nigel Smith (Raintree, 2002)

Websites

http://www.ironbridge.org.uk

http://www.sciencemuseum.org.uk

http://www.amberleymuseum.co.uk

Note to parents and teachers: Every effort has been made by the publishers to ensure that these websites are suitable for children. However, because of the nature of the Internet, it is impossible to guarantee that the contents of these sites will not be altered. We strongly advise that Internet access is supervised by a responsible adult.

Places to visit

The Ironbridge Gorge Museum Trust, Coach Road, Coalbrookdale, Telford, TF8 7DQ

The North of England Open Air Museum, Beamish, County Durham, DH9 0RG

The Science Museum, Exhibition Road, London, SW7 2DD

The National Rail Museum, Leeman Road, York, YO26 WXJ

Amberley Working Museum, Amberley, West Sussex, BN18 9LT

SS Great Britain, Great Western Dockyard, Gas Ferry Road, Bristol, BS1 6TY

Museum of Science and Industry, Liverpool Road, Castlefield, Manchester, M3 4FP

Index